ORGANIZE YOUR LIFE IN A WEEKEND

ORGANIZE YOUR LIFE IN A WEEKEND

SERAPHINA WILDE

CONTENTS

CHAPTER 1

Introduction

Welcome to a weekend that could change your life. This process isn't about cleaning and beautification—it's about decluttering and organizing with ruthless efficiency. Let's be honest, it's going to get messy. You might stumble upon a Halloween mask from 1998 in a box alongside your children's artwork from two years ago. Spoiler alert: we won't get to that today. Our goal is to eliminate everything disposable immediately and categorize the rest in a way that makes it easy to maintain.

Before we dive in, take a moment to understand the core reasons behind organizing. This will help you stay motivated and recognize the value in what you're about to undertake.

It's mid-January, and I'm already weary of the endless tips on "organizing" for the New Year. Why am I writing yet another guide? Because most of the advice I've come across is overly ambitious for a quick start guide to organizing your life in just one weekend. Here I am, offering a practical, no-nonsense alternative for anyone determined to get it done in two days.

Yes, it is possible. No, you won't be sleeping much. But if you can commit 12-24 hours of your weekend to this, I promise it will transform your home, work, relationships, and stress levels. Ready to pay the price for a better tomorrow? So am I.

CHAPTER 2

Assessing Your Current Situation

Who are you, and what do you need? Do you crave physical activity, intellectual stimulation, or emotional rewards? I had friends who remarried, blending their families. Their combined kids wanted what any child would desire: a happy family, good food, a warm light in a cozy home. Many families today are like my friends'—they need things to run smoothly but without turning family members into robots. Plans are made, but often the universe sticks to its own secret timetable. Maybe a child gets sick during your rare downtime, or you catch a cold, or something unexpected happens. Life is unpredictable.

It's essential to ensure your life brings you joy in the ways you desire. If you haven't taken a good, honest look at what you need to be happy, now is the time. How organized are you in this aspect of your life? Wanting something is only half the battle; you must also figure out how to achieve it. Are you standing in your own way? (Hint: the answer is probably "Yes.")

Ask yourself: What's working and what isn't in your life? What's dragging you down and what's pushing you forward? Identifying your biggest challenges can feel overwhelming, but it's also liberating. Seeing everything laid out can help put things into perspective. When a car breaks down in a snowstorm, you don't focus on clearing the driveway; you focus on getting the car out. Apply the same logic to your problems.

Although I joke about people who make lists, they are incredibly useful. Lists are to-do markers—empowering tools. The moment you write down what's wrong, a light begins to flicker in the darkness. Suddenly, you have a target to attack. There's no need to make a list right now; we'll get to that later. For now, let's avoid peaking too soon. Sit tight, and let's continue this journey together.

CHAPTER 3

Setting Goals and Priorities

Let's talk about setting goals and priorities. Many people list their tasks and then rank them by importance. Respecting this list often means putting what's important—like exercise, sleep, decluttering, fun, and rest—before what's urgent for others, such as cooking, cleaning, and charging the phone. Those who don't follow lists and priorities often feel overwhelmed. They lack time for things they find interesting and important, miss out on good rest, are constantly on the run, and experience growing stress.

To redirect our lives effectively, we need to take a step back and evaluate what isn't working. It's crucial to reassess periodically to ensure we're moving toward our goals. Answer the following questions honestly: What would you love to do but can't find the time for? What would you love to buy but can't find the money for? What else in life should you invest in or learn about to have clearer ideas about your true goals?

Don't try to change too many things at once. Instead, build a plan to redirect yourself with a promise to follow your intuition.

Identifying what's dragging you down and what's pushing you forward is essential. Understanding your biggest challenges can feel overwhelming but also liberating. When everything is laid out in front of you, it helps put things into perspective. Just like focusing on getting your car out when it breaks down in a snowstorm, focus on tackling your problems methodically.

Lists are powerful tools for achieving this. Although I joke about people who make lists, they are incredibly useful. Lists are empowering to-do markers. Writing down what's wrong is the first step towards finding solutions. Suddenly, you have a target to attack. We'll make a detailed list later, so for now, let's avoid peaking too soon. Sit tight, and let's continue this journey together.

CHAPTER 4

Creating a Schedule

Think of creating a schedule as you would a recipe—it can be improved and developed from scratch. An effective schedule helps you function at your peak without necessarily filling every second of your day. Let's keep it simple. Visualize your 24-hour day in slices of time, from when you wake up to when you go to bed. Each slice of time may be different.

Take, for example, maintaining a blissful, loving relationship. It's generally understood that you should spend at least 15 hours per week with your significant other, and vice versa, to keep your relationship flourishing. These 30 hours can be integrated into your monthly schedule in 2-hour blocks daily. So, 1.25 hours should be added to your daily schedule early in the day (6am-8am) and 1.25 hours should be added late in the day (8pm-10pm).

No matter how free-spirited you are, everything and everyone in this world operates based on time. Creation, destruction, and change all happen within time. Therefore, understanding time in your personal life is crucial. Scheduling is important because virtually everything can be scheduled, at least roughly. You sleep at certain times, commute at specific times, attend meetings, classes, and workshops at scheduled times, and meet family and friends at planned times. Time, therefore, is a significant variable in your life.

CHAPTER 5

Decluttering and Organizing Your Space

Decluttering is perhaps the biggest and most time-consuming task, but it is absolutely essential. Not only does it allow you to own less, but it also promotes better organization, increases energy levels, and reduces anxiety. You owe it to yourself to do more than just maintain the status quo in your environment. Constantly deciding to keep things as they are is exhausting. Instead, invest the effort once to overhaul your space, and then it's done. You won't have to devote the huge amount of time and effort it takes to keep your space in order ever again. Just let that sink in for a minute.

Do you ever feel like life happens to you rather than something you actively participate in? Do you feel out of control of your space and time, like your house is a mess, your schedule is constantly booked, and you're always looking for something, even though you're not sure what "it" is? I used to feel quite lost, out of control, and paralyzed with indecision, so I understand this area well. It doesn't have to be this way.

You don't need to overhaul your entire life to achieve necessary self-organization goals. In just one weekend, you can create incredible motivation for change within yourself. By decluttering and organizing your space, you set the stage for a more controlled and fulfilling life.

Here's how to get started:

1. **Set Clear Goals**: Identify the areas in your home that need the most attention. Start with spaces that impact your daily life, like your kitchen, bedroom, or workspace.
2. **Create a Plan**: Break the task into manageable chunks. Decide what to tackle first and allocate specific times to each area.
3. **Sort and Categorize**: Use boxes or bins to sort items into categories such as 'Keep', 'Donate', 'Recycle', and 'Trash'. This will help you make quick decisions and keep the process moving.
4. **Deep Clean**: Once you've decluttered, give each area a thorough cleaning. This will make the space feel fresh and new.
5. **Organize Intuitively**: Arrange the items you're keeping in a way that makes sense to you. Use storage solutions that work with your space and lifestyle.
6. **Maintain**: Develop simple habits to keep your space organized. Spend a few minutes each day tidying up, and regularly assess what you have to prevent clutter from building up again.

Remember, the goal is to create a space that supports your life and brings you joy. By investing time and effort now, you'll save yourself from ongoing stress and chaos.

CHAPTER 6

Streamlining Your Daily Routine

The key to a successful daily routine is designing a sequence that triggers habits, allowing you to perform many tasks with minimal conscious thought. Routines are efficient mechanisms for managing productivity because their predictability frees up mental capacity for more complex tasks. A typical sequence might include showering, drinking a glass of water, brushing your teeth, meditating, preparing your bag, and blending meal replacements. Using this cycle as a tool, you can create time slots and fill them with your daily routine. Remember, the objective is to improve your routine to better fit your lifestyle, not to make it perfect for everyone. It should help you get through the day and allow you to focus on tasks outside of your routine.

Streamlining your daily routine means faithfully following a sequence of tasks that will trigger habits, breaking them down into manageable parts, which will eventually become automatic. The exact sequence of tasks is up to you, as it should reflect your lifestyle, responsibilities, and priorities. There's no need to time your routine precisely, but having a rough idea of how long it should take—25 minutes, 50 minutes, an hour—can be helpful. You can then combine your routine with a time increment to form a cycle, your planning unit. This way, you'll be planning and accomplishing each cycle, with short breaks to attend to various aspects of your life.

Living by default means letting time and others make your plans for you. It means appearing busy and running from crisis to crisis without achieving anything significant. Reacting instead of planning. In contrast, living by design offers the opportunity to live life on your terms, balancing work, family, personal interests, and physical and mental health. Balancing different aspects of your life is crucial for overall well-being, as they are interconnected.

Plan your time to get things done rather than simply pursuing goals. Be the owner and creator of your days. Be the source of your happiness, not dependent on anyone or anything else. Deal with each moment as it comes, without letting external factors dictate your response.

CHAPTER 7

Managing Your Finances

After eight years of being self-employed and trying to figure out how to have a healthy relationship with my finances—something that definitely did not come naturally to me—I was at the end of my rope. Then a friend shared an eye-opening article titled "Want to Change How You Think About Money? Procrastinate." It described how two MIT economists taught people to be accountable with their money using piles. People separated their money into stacks and labeled them—rent, groceries, etc. This method sounded doable, so I gave it a try.

In fact, I made elegant piles with a magic marker. And you know what? It worked. For the past year, I haven't been worried about money at all. I actually feel good about doing it—unlike my usual pretzelicious feelings about finances. I know I'm not the only one struggling with this, so I'm passing this along. Check it out and see if it might work for you too! Keep doing whatever feels good and isn't torturous. Take baby steps until you're comfortable with the accountability part. The more sustainable your strategy, the less willpower you'll need. And we all know willpower doesn't work in the long run anyway.

For many of us, managing finances is the least appealing part of getting organized. But it can also have the most significant and immediate benefits. "Wallet fatigue" chews away at our attention, energy, and ability to make good decisions. The money and time it costs us are simply not worth it. Ironically, although finances can be one of the hardest things to manage, you don't have to do everything all at once. Start small and keep baby-stepping.

The big secret to keeping organized and accountable with your money until it becomes a healthy habit is to adopt a system that feels doable and non-torturous. Here are some steps to help you manage your finances:

1. **Categorize Your Money**: Separate your money into categories such as rent, groceries, entertainment, and savings. Label each category clearly.
2. **Create a Budget**: Outline your monthly income and expenses. Allocate funds to each category based on your needs and priorities.
3. **Track Your Spending**: Keep a record of your expenses. This will help you stay accountable and identify areas where you can cut back.
4. **Set Financial Goals**: Define short-term and long-term financial goals. Whether it's saving for a vacation, paying off debt, or building an emergency fund, having clear goals will motivate you to stay on track.
5. **Automate Savings**: Set up automatic transfers to your savings account. This ensures you consistently save money without having to think about it.
6. **Review and Adjust**: Regularly review your budget and spending. Adjust as necessary to accommodate changes in your financial situation.

Remember, managing your finances doesn't have to be overwhelming. Start small, take baby steps, and gradually build a system that works for you. The key is consistency and finding a method that feels sustainable and non-torturous.

CHAPTER 8

Establishing Healthy Habits

Do you find it challenging to unwind before going to sleep? Are you going to bed and waking up at different times each day? Are there avoidable negative factors impacting your chances of a restful night's sleep? Once you evaluate these factors, work on eliminating all avoidable sleep enemies. Then, establish a night routine that will give your body and mind the runway to land for the night. This should include activities that help you unwind and relax, preferably away from screens.

Aim to keep these habits at the same time every day, even on weekends and during holidays. When your days fall into a regular rhythm, your body (especially your brain) will recognize the routine and facilitate easier sleep. This will take time and some tweaking as you discover what works and what doesn't for you. Did you know that the half-hour before you sleep is typically the most crucial time to be in darkness for better sleep? This is why establishing good habits around your evening routine and learning how to wind down is essential. A good night's sleep might await if you follow these tips.

Our bodies operate on cycles, typically around 24 hours. The body and brain need a consistent amount of sleep at the same time daily to feel rested and focused. Establishing healthy sleep patterns and habits is crucial for a healthy lifestyle. Most adults require 7+ hours of good quality sleep each night.

Start by ensuring your sleeping space is conducive to rest. Do an audit of your sleeping area:

- **Eliminate Distractions**: Are there electronic devices that could distract you?
- **Create Darkness**: Is the room dark enough?
- **Ensure Comfort**: Are you comfortable and at the right temperature, not too hot or cold?

Once your space is in good shape, assess your personal sleep problems and work on addressing them. Here are some tips to help you establish a healthy sleep routine:

1. **Set a Consistent Schedule**: Go to bed and wake up at the same times every day.
2. **Create a Relaxing Pre-Sleep Routine**: Engage in calming activities, such as reading, meditating, or taking a warm bath.
3. **Avoid Screens Before Bed**: Minimize exposure to screens at least an hour before bedtime.
4. **Limit Caffeine and Alcohol**: Avoid consuming caffeine or alcohol close to bedtime.
5. **Make Your Sleep Environment Comfortable**: Ensure your mattress and pillows are comfortable, and your room is quiet and dark.

Establishing these habits can improve your overall health and well-being, making your daily life more enjoyable and productive.

CHAPTER 9

Building a Support System

Building a sturdy support system is essential for maintaining your organized path. Before you enlist anyone else to be in your army, talk to them about the type of support you need. Whether you want someone to challenge you, coach you, or just listen to your dilemmas, make sure they feel comfortable in that role. The type of support you need may not be comfortable for them, in which case they won't be up to the task when you need them. Conversely, if the person you wanted as a rah-rah coach only wanted to be an empathetic listener, you've set yourself up for disappointment.

Here are some tips to build a strong support system:

1. **Set and Clarify Your Goals**: Share your goals with your support system. Someone might offer ideas you hadn't considered. Sharing your goals also makes you more accountable, as more people are aware of them.
2. **Be a Gentle Taskmaster**: If you promised to walk daily, the guilt of having to tell someone, "I blew it off again today," may be all you need to get out the door.

3. **Share Stress**: Talking to someone can help you navigate confusion and uncertainty. Sharing the burden of stress can provide relief.
4. **Get Encouragement**: Your support group can cheer you on to victory. Celebrating and sharing your successes with others is much more fun.

You can organize your physical space, set goals, and find energy. You are on a roll. You think, "I can do this!" But will you? The energy you feel now may wane temporarily. How can you keep on your organized path? Just as you maximized your time by doing several organizing projects at once, you can maximize your energy and enthusiasm by building a strong support system.

The most successful people in any field have support systems. Even the Lone Ranger had Tonto. A support system can help you:

- **Stay Accountable**: Regular check-ins with your support group can keep you accountable and motivated to stick with your goals.
- **Provide Perspective**: Friends and family can offer different perspectives and insights, helping you see challenges and solutions you might have missed.
- **Offer Emotional Support**: Knowing you have people who care about your well-being can boost your morale and emotional resilience.

Remember, building a support system is about creating a network of people who understand your goals and are willing to support you in achieving them. By doing this, you'll be better equipped to stay organized and maintain your progress.

CHAPTER 10

Time Management Techniques

Working on your task list might make you think about your jobs and cause nervousness or a loss of confidence. Over time, we often fool ourselves into believing we can handle multiple tasks simultaneously. However, this is a misconception, as multitasking leads to doing tasks poorly. I've spent thousands of hours building plans in my profession and felt ashamed at times. Some tactics are better than others, and certain routines can help you gain time every day. If you reflect on your workday and find a way to save just one hour per day, you gain ten weeks per year. Isn't it worth investing an hour on Friday to save an hour each day? Overwhelming tasks can make us rush, but putting your plans on paper can help. Everything is allowed except blank plans. Remember, there's no pressure for perfect plans. Start directly, and reap the real benefits at once.

Doing ten things at once won't work. Humans believe in multitasking, but our brains can only handle one task at a time efficiently. The prefrontal cortex, the thinking part of the brain, is slow. Shifting attention from one task to another isn't automatic, and our brains aren't designed to do this quickly. We waste time. Imagine trying to build a house by placing a brick on ten different spots simultaneously—it's impossible. Instead, focus on one task at a time to get things done.

Here are some effective time management techniques:

1. **Prioritize Tasks**: Identify the most important tasks and tackle them first. Use tools like the Eisenhower Matrix to categorize tasks by urgency and importance.
2. **Set Clear Goals**: Define what you want to achieve each day. Having clear goals helps you stay focused and motivated.
3. **Use a To-Do List**: A to-do list helps you remember tasks and prioritize them. Digitalize your to-dos for easier management with a task management app.
4. **Time Blocking**: Allocate specific time slots for each task. This prevents multitasking and allows you to focus on one task at a time.
5. **Avoid Distractions**: Identify and minimize distractions. Create a work environment that supports concentration.
6. **Take Breaks**: Regular breaks prevent burnout and increase productivity. Use techniques like the Pomodoro Technique, which involves working for 25 minutes and then taking a 5-minute break.
7. **Reflect and Adjust**: At the end of each day, reflect on what worked and what didn't. Adjust your plans accordingly for the next day.

Living by default means letting time and others dictate your plans, leading to constant busyness without achieving much. Reacting instead of planning. In contrast, living by design allows you to live life on your terms, balancing work, family, personal interests, and health. Balancing different aspects of your life is crucial for overall well-being.

Plan your time to accomplish tasks, not just pursue goals. Be the creator of your days. Deal with each moment as it comes, without letting external factors dictate your response.

CHAPTER 11

Maximizing Productivity

Creating a daily goal book can help you use your time effectively. The key is to allocate specific amounts of time to the activities you've identified as important. Remember, your time is your only non-renewable asset! Always approach your time management with the mindset that planning is crucial to success. Before you start anything, develop an efficient system tailored to your needs. This system should include what goes in, what goes out, and what's left of your resources.

Here's how you can structure your daily goal book:

1. **Specific, Attainable, and Measurable Goals**: Make your goals detailed yet flexible. Clearly define what you want to achieve.
2. **Daily Breakdown**: Use a page-a-day format to schedule events, appointments, classes, work shifts, etc.
3. **Action Steps**: Outline what you must do now to achieve your goals later. Break these into manageable steps.
4. **Mini Goals**: Set mini goals for the day, week, and month to easily track your progress.
5. **Critical Tasks**: Identify tasks that need to be sorted out before you can make further objective decisions.

6. **Budget and Spending**: Include a section for planning any purchases. Determine if these purchases are feasible.

When you organize your space and your work, you maximize productivity by writing down your goals in a daily goal book and following through with a plan that puts those goals into action. At a glance, you will know how to allocate your valuable time each day. Having a daily written plan ensures you don't miss a step.

A daily goal book should contain:

- **Specific, Attainable, and Measurable Goals**: Clearly define your goals, making them detailed but flexible.
- **Daily Schedule**: Breakdown of scheduled events, appointments, classes, work shifts, etc.
- **Action Steps**: Steps to achieve your goals, broken down into manageable tasks.
- **Mini Goals**: Daily, weekly, and monthly goals to track your progress.
- **Critical Tasks**: Tasks that need to be addressed before making further decisions.
- **Budget and Spending**: Plan for any purchases, ensuring they are feasible.

By jotting down your goals and following a structured plan, you can maximize your productivity. Your daily goal book will guide you in allocating your valuable time effectively and help you stay on track to achieve your objectives.

CHAPTER 12

Developing Effective Communication Skills

Effective communication is a cornerstone of successful relationships, work environments, and leadership. One key aspect of communication is active listening. The pyramid of listening will help improve our capability for effective and active listening. Listening actively means decoding the message and providing feedback to the interlocutor. We listen for comprehension, interpretation, and to capture the essence of what we hear. Then, we form our response based on that essence, providing genuine attention to the conversational partner. It is crucial to use this approach for good communication, especially in areas influencing our private and work lives.

Don't just hear your interlocutor, listen to them. Stellar communicators know how to use mirroring techniques to find congruence with the person in front of them and can use direct and precise questions to probe an issue in depth. Effective use of intermittent sounds such as "I see," "mmm," and "I understand" facilitates communication and helps maintain the audience's attention. Remember, communication only occurs if someone is willing to listen. If you can't focus, it's impossible to communicate effectively.

To better manage the content of our communication, it is essential to establish the rules for effective conversation and recognize how often we can ignore them. This information will improve our understanding of efficient dialogues and help explain why so many of our arguments become heated and go off track.

Stellar communication skills improve our interrelationships, work environment, and effectiveness as leaders. Effective communication combines a set of complex and integral skills:

1. **Listening**: Truly understand and decode the message being communicated.
2. **Non-Verbal Communication**: Gestures, body language, and facial expressions play a significant role in conveying messages.
3. **Questioning**: Ask direct and precise questions to delve deeper into issues.
4. **Paraphrasing**: Restate what you've heard to ensure comprehension and show you're listening.
5. **Recognizing Unproductive Patterns**: Identify and avoid patterns that lead to misunderstandings or conflicts.

Integrating these skills helps us become more effective speakers and listeners. Here's how you can develop and hone these skills:

- **Practice Active Listening**: Focus entirely on the speaker, avoid interrupting, and respond thoughtfully.
- **Use Positive Body Language**: Maintain eye contact, nod, and use open gestures.
- **Ask Clarifying Questions**: Don't be afraid to ask questions if you don't understand something.

- **Paraphrase for Clarity**: Summarize what the speaker has said in your own words to ensure understanding.
- **Be Mindful of Non-Verbal Cues**: Pay attention to your own and others' body language and adjust accordingly.
- **Avoid Unproductive Communication Patterns**: Recognize and break habits that lead to conflict or miscommunication.

Developing these skills will enhance your ability to connect with others, resolve conflicts, and lead effectively.

Simplifying Decision Making

Simplifying decision-making can significantly impact various areas of your life positively. Often, when people hear about the concept of mental clarity, they recognize this urge within themselves—regardless of whether they come from a place of abundance or scarcity. The idea of simplifying is handed to them in one neat package, including all the things they thought they could never give up. Sometimes, we set a mental trap for ourselves, thinking we must genuinely commit to cleansing to pursue it. Then, we try to deduce if that would satisfy us, ultimately telling ourselves we can't do it.

This step in simplifying decision-making can help you reduce mental clutter and stress. When you don't have to choose between four or five similar shampoo bottles on a shelf or color coordinate thirty different t-shirts, you're better suited to make affirmative decisions when you actually need to.

As the mental and emotional load of multitasking, demanding routines, and countless distractions build up, we accumulate mental clutter that stresses us out. Our brain yearns for clarity and simplicity, but the very idea of unloading an inordinate amount of things all at once can feel overwhelming. Here are some strategies to help simplify your decision-making process:

1. **Reduce Options**: Limit the number of choices you have to make daily. Fewer options mean less mental energy spent on making decisions. For example, streamline your wardrobe to a few versatile pieces.

2. **Set Clear Criteria**: Define clear criteria for making decisions. Knowing your priorities and values will guide you in making choices that align with your goals.

3. **Create Routines**: Establish routines for everyday tasks. This reduces the number of decisions you need to make daily, freeing up mental space for more critical decisions.

4. **Delegate Decisions**: Whenever possible, delegate decisions to others. Trusting your team or family to handle specific tasks can reduce your mental load.

5. **Use Decision-Making Tools**: Utilize tools like decision matrices or pros and cons lists to evaluate your options systematically.

6. **Practice Mindfulness**: Stay present and focused. Mindfulness can help you avoid overthinking and make decisions more confidently.

By adopting these strategies, you can simplify your decision-making process, reduce mental clutter, and improve your overall quality of life. Remember, the goal is to create a sense of mental clarity that allows you to focus on what truly matters.

CHAPTER 14

Maintaining Long-Term Organization

To maintain your organizational system, it's essential to give it the same attention you give to your devices and furniture. Your phone needs regular updates to keep functioning, and even your custom desk might need some reinforcement after taking a few hits. Your shelving can only hold so much before it gives out. Even your backup system could become obsolete. Investing in a couple of high-capacity jump drives or a large hard drive might not be as long-lasting as paying for a decent hard drive with online storage. Reevaluate your system periodically to see how it's holding up. Recheck your setup to ensure it still suits your current needs and add a few reminders to your system for maintenance tasks.

Every organizational system requires some maintenance. Even space shuttles need updates with new parts or software, and their components must remain in working order to ensure a safe journey. While you might not be flying to the moon, you still need to maintain your system. Handle the paper or new items that gather in your home or workspace regularly. It's normal for this to happen, and it's okay. Dealing with them once a week or once a day can keep them from taking over your space. Always remember the "one in, one out" concept. Not only does it help prevent an excess of items, but it also helps manage the mess left behind.

Here are some tips for maintaining long-term organization:

1. **Regularly Review Your System**: Periodically evaluate your organizational system to ensure it still meets your needs. Adjust as necessary to accommodate changes in your life.
2. **Update Your Tools and Technology**: Keep your organizational tools and technology updated. This includes software updates for your devices and replacing any worn-out equipment.
3. **Handle New Items Promptly**: Address new items that come into your space regularly. This prevents clutter from building up and keeps your system functioning smoothly.
4. **Follow the "One In, One Out" Rule**: For every new item you bring in, remove an old one. This helps maintain balance and prevents excessive accumulation.
5. **Set Reminders**: Use reminders to prompt you to perform regular maintenance tasks. This ensures you don't overlook necessary updates and clean-ups.
6. **Stay Flexible**: Be willing to adapt your system as your needs change. Flexibility is key to maintaining long-term organization.

By following these tips and regularly maintaining your system, you can keep your space organized and functional for the long term. Consistent maintenance will save you time and effort in the long run, ensuring that your organizational efforts remain effective.

CHAPTER 15

Celebrating Your Accomplishments

To help you get into a positive habit for your ongoing journey to get organized, take a little time to celebrate everything you've just achieved. I mean that sincerely. You've just taken a significant step forward to improve the quality of your life. You deserve to enjoy a goofy dance in your living room or spend time reflecting on how far you've come. If you're the kind of person who enjoys giving yourself credit (and why not!), be sure to write it down in your weekly progress journal. You might even want to celebrate your progress with some automated recognition in your online to-do list.

Life can sometimes seem like a never-ending to-do list. As mentioned in the introduction, it's easy to get ahead of yourself and feel overwhelmed by everything you want to achieve. While this book's primary purpose is to help you jump-start organizing your life, it's also important to note that organizing your life is an ongoing event. It's not as though we reach a point of Nirvana where everything runs itself. If only that were the case—it would be spectacular!

Remember to celebrate your accomplishments, no matter how small. Recognizing your progress can boost your motivation and keep you moving forward. Here are some ways to celebrate your achievements:

1. **Reflect on Your Progress**: Take a moment to look back at what you've achieved. Acknowledge your hard work and dedication.
2. **Reward Yourself**: Treat yourself to something you enjoy, whether it's a favorite meal, a relaxing spa day, or a new book.
3. **Share Your Success**: Tell a friend or family member about your accomplishments. Sharing your success can make it feel more real and rewarding.
4. **Document Your Achievements**: Keep a journal or digital record of your accomplishments. This will serve as a reminder of your progress and motivate you to keep going.
5. **Set New Goals**: Use your accomplishments as a stepping stone to set new, exciting goals. Celebrate the journey, not just the destination.

By taking the time to celebrate your accomplishments, you reinforce positive habits and create a sense of fulfillment. Remember, the journey to an organized life is ongoing, and each step forward is worth celebrating.

Conclusion

So, did minimalism do what it's meant to do and declutter your life in a weekend? I suspect it didn't take 48 hours to completely organize your entire bedroom, but now you have the momentum and a clear starting point. Simply starting puts you miles ahead of everyone who says they'll do it "someday," but never do. As Martin Luther King Jr. once said, "You don't have to see the whole staircase, just take the first step." Go ahead, make a positive impact in the world, and I'll meet you at the top.

Reflecting on the past two days, you've organized everything from your physical belongings to your computer desktop and calendar. This physical purge, technological cleanse, and thought explosion will allow you to move forward in peace, focusing on what's most important to you. As with any guide on minimalism (and life), always tailor the process to fit your lifestyle; it's not a one-size-fits-all solution. This is just the beginning. Moving forward, strive to maintain a clear headspace and tidy environment. Don't forget to put in the effort to evolve continuously over time if you find yourself out of sync. Our routines change, our interests shift; this will lead to future purges and decluttering.

Remember, maintaining an organized life is an ongoing journey. It's about making choices every day that align with your goals and values. Celebrate your progress, embrace the changes, and keep moving forward. The journey to an organized life is unique for each person, but the rewards are universal—less stress, more focus, and a greater sense of peace.

Congratulations on taking the first step towards a more organized and fulfilling life. Keep going, keep evolving, and enjoy the journey.